Loretta Santini - Cinzia Valigi

CITIES OF ITALY

SPOLETO

GUIDE WITH PLAN

CENTRO STAMPA EDITORIALE

plurigraf

PERSEUS

PG-S

Spoleto

The beautiful Umbrian town of Spoleto attracts tourists from all over the world with its artistic heritage and cultural events of the highest standard.

Spread in a cluster over gently-sloping hills and dominated by its imposing and historical fortress and the densely-wooded slopes of Monteluco behind it, Spoleto is more richly endowed with monuments from the past, especially from the medieval period, than most other towns in Umbria, even in Italy.

Spoleto is an unforgettable town not only for its beauty but also because it has become the venue for an annual Arts Festival of international stature called the "Festival of the Two Worlds" and for important conferences, such as the Congresses on the Early Middle Ages, held in the town every year.

Spoleto's history is a distinguished one. Founded in prehistoric times, it was occupied by the ancient Umbrians, under whom it rose to political power and economic importance. It later became a flourishing and splendid Roman town with the name of Spoletium (a name of Etruscan origin, suggesting a temporary ascendancy of the Etruscan civilization over this area).

Spoleto was occupied by the Lombards and then, in the 6th century, became the capital of the Duchy of Spoleto which rapidly rose to such great political importance that its dukes aspired to the imperial crown itself. It was during the same period that the town extended its rule over the surrounding territory until a large part of Central Italy lay under its control.

Weakened by the major defeat inflicted on it by Frederick Barbarossa, Spoleto came under the control of the Papal States from the 12th century onwards. In the ensuing period it was torn by continuous civil strife and was characterized by alternating periods of greater or lesser splendour and importance. Essentially, its history was not dissimilar from that of many other Umbrian towns, though it somehow always maintained a pre-eminent historical and cultural role.

Spoleto and the Festival of the two Worlds

The Festival of the Two Worlds (Festival dei Due Mondi), founded by Giancarlo Menotti in 1958 and held in Spoleto every year in the last few days of June and the first few days of July, may undoubtedly be ranked among the most important and prestigious cultural events to take place on the international scene every year.

It offers a wide range of exhibitions, ballet, opera, plays and concerts, all of them of the highest standard and performed, conducted and directed by major international figures of long-standing fame or by avant-garde companies that have succeeded in making an original and important contribution to the performing arts. The gala concert held on the final day of the Festival against the magnificent backdrop of the Cathedral is particularly renowned. Numerous conductors, dancers and actors have established their reputation during the Spoleto Festivals, obtaining lasting fame and success thanks both to their professional skill and talent and to the prestige of the Festival, renowned for its selectivity and for the high standards it demands of all who take part in it. The Festival is important too for inviting representatives from different schools, techniques and styles from all over the world, thus bringing together widely divergent artistic experiences. In the delightful theatres and in the picturesque squares of the town, in an ideal setting rich in memories of the past and in magnificent monuments marked by the patina of time, shrouded in a quiet and intimate atmosphere reminiscent of the Middle Ages, both old and new works have been performed, and both artistes of long-standing fame and young artistes who are less well known but just as gifted, and able to bring new and interesting ideas to the fore, have taken their turn on the stage.

Scenes from two ballets performed during the Festival of the Two Worlds, in which opera, ballet and musical performances of the highest quality are given every year.

Concert on the final day of the Festival in the Cathedral Square.

View of Spoleto from Collerisana. The fortress, towers and rooftops of the town stand out against the densely-wooded slopes of Monteluco,

towering in the background. The Borgo San Matteo (St.Matthew's district), called the "Borgaccio", can be seen in the foreground.

THE CATHEDRAL OF OUR LADY OF THE ASSUMPTION
(SANTA MARIA ASSUNTA)

A masterpiece of architecture, the splendid Cathedral of Our Lady of the Assumption is a combination of various styles which testify to the different stages of its construction, but somehow succeed in blending together in a harmonious whole. The building even incorporates materials dating from the Roman period, visible in the bell-tower. The main structure of the Cathedral is, however, medieval, as is particularly obvious from its façade, although the

elegant portico in front of it dates from the Renaissance. The Cathedral is situated at the far end of the square bearing its name (Piazza del Duomo), and forms the backdrop to the gala concert with which the town's Arts Festival comes to a close each year. The façade is of particular architectural interest: it is divided into three vertical sections by pilaster strips, decorated by slightly pointed arches and a number of rose windows. At the centre of the façade, an elegant doorway leads into the nave. Above, a large mosaic of Christ occupies the central arch of the upper section.

The portico in front of the Cathedral, with its five arches, was designed by Antonio Barocci and Pippo Di Antonio, and blends elegantly with the Romanesque façade. At each end of the portico there are two finely-sculpted pulpits (see photo below right). The interior of the Cathedral contains a series of splendid works of art. Particularly worthy of note are the frescoes in the apse painted by the Florentine artist Filippo Lippi, which are a masterpiece of Renaissance art. Paintings by Pinturicchio, a statue of Pope Urban VIII by Bernini and a fine Byzantine icon venerated in the Chapel of the Holy Icon may also be admired.

In the right transept is the tomb of Filippo Lippi, who frescoed the apse of the church. A number of important documents and an autograph of St. Francis of Assisi are preserved in the adjoining presbytery.

Chapel of Relics - altar crucifix by Alberto Sozio (1187)

Cathedral - the apse is decorated with splendid frescoes depicting stories from the life of the Virgin, which Filippo Lippi painted between 1467 and 1469, just before he died. In the fresco shown on this page, depicting "The Death of Mary", the artist has painted a portrait of himself, with his son beside him, and of the artists who helped him: Fra' Diamante and Pier Matteo d'Amelia. A 14th century wooden statue of the Madonna and Child; the work of an unknown Umbrian sculptor, is kept in the Chapel of Relics.

13

"Nativity" - This was the last fresco to be completed, and was painted almost entirely by Lippi's assistants, Fra' Diamante and Pier Matteo d'Amelia.
In the vault of the apse, "Coronation of the Virgin", a beautiful and intensely mystical fresco by Filippo Lippi (photo on next page).

Cathedral - frescoes from the apse. On the apse wall, Annunciation". This fresco by Filippo Lippi is one of the most expressive in the whole cycle; particularly worthy of note is the delicate and melancholy expression on the Virgin's face which the painter has succeeded in conveying.

Cathedral - "Madonna and Child" - detail.

In the Chapel of Bishop Costantino Eroli there is a splendid fresco portraying the "Madonna and Child with St.John the Baptist and St. Leonard" by Pinturicchio.

18

CHURCH OF OUR LADY OF THE GOLDEN MANNA
(SANTA MARIA DELLA MANNA D'ORO)

The Church of Our Lady of the Golden Manna stands beside the Cathedral. Built between the 16th and 17th centuries, it was dedicated to the Virgin by the people of Spoleto after the Sack of Rome in 1527. The church, octagonal in shape, is in the style typical of the famous 15th century architect, Bramante. Inside, a statue of Bishop Bernardino Lauri and four paintings by Sebastiano Conca and Nicola Costantini are kept. In the middle of the church is a 15th century baptismal font which came from the Eroli Chapel in the Cathedral. To the left of the church stand the Caio Melisso Theatre and the Municipal Museum.

◄ Via dell'Arringo

MUNICIPAL MUSEUM
(MUSEO CIVICO)

Situated on the first floor of the 14th century building called the Palazzo della Signoria, the Municipal Museum was set up during the first decade of this century by the archaeologist G. Sordini, and contains an interesting archaeological collection as well as medieval and Renaissance sculptures. The most important exhibits include: the sarcophagus of St Isaac dating from the 12th century (above), several capitals and statues, two Renaissance ciboria and two tablets dating from the 3rd century B.C. inscribed with the order not to cut down trees in two woods of the Spoleto Valley which were considered sacred.

16th century tabernacle with a bas-relief depicting Christ in the tomb (lunette) and the Grief of Christ (door).

Municipal Museum - Bas-relief depicting scenes of the martyrdom of St. Biagio.

CAIO MELISSO THEATRE - This theatre stands next to the Church of Our Lady of the Golden Manna. First built in the 17th century, it was originally called the Nobile Theatre after a distinguished townsman of Spoleto. Later, around the middle of the 18th century, the theatre was embellished with paintings and sculptures. Rebuilt in the 19th century by the architect Giovanni Montiroli, it was named after the playwright of Roman times, Caio Melisso, who was born in Spoleto and was a friend of Maecenas and the Emperor Augustus. The fine ceiling with a depiction of Apollo and the Muses and the curtain portraying Caio Melisso's Gloria are the work of D. Bruschi.

Via dell'Arringo

Church of St.Euphemia - outside view of the apse

CHURCH OF ST EUPHEMIA (SANT'EUFEMIA)

The entrance to St.Euphemia's Church is located in the courtyard of the Archbishop's Palace. The church is a fine and extremely interesting example of Romanesque architecture. Restored between 1907 and 1953, the façade is decorated by pilaster strips, hanging arches and two single-arched windows of Lombard Romanesque style. The two sloping roofs on either side of the façade which lead up to the central raised section, the doorway surrounded by concentric arches and the flying buttresses are all typical of the early Romanesque style in Spoleto. The horizontal ledge half-way up the façade, and the column and capital of the central, double-arched window are not original, but the result of restoration work. The interior of the church, small and harmonious in its proportions, is split into three naves distinguished by their pronounced verticality. The alternating columns and pillars are partly made up of elements from other buildings from Roman or early medieval times. Overlooking the central nave is the women's gallery, which in the past was reserved for the nuns of the convent which once existed. The beautiful marble-fronted main altar dates back to the 13th century. The church still contains several fine paintings.

Church of St.Euphemia - interior

Via di Visiale, a typical medieval street with arches connecting the buildings on either side.

Typical narrow street

Town Hall

ROMAN HOUSE

Underneath the Town Hall (Palazzo Comunale) there are the remains of a Roman house, dating back to the 1st century A.D., which would seem, according to an inscription, to have belonged to Vespasia

Polla, mother of the Emperor Vespasian. At the centre of the house is the impluvium, surrounded by the bedrooms and triclinium; to the left is the peristyle. The floor mosaics are worthy of note.

MUNICIPAL PICTURE GALLERY (PINACOTECA COMUNALE)

The Municipal Picture Gallery is situated on the first floor of the Town Hall. Spread over various rooms, it contains numerous objects of artistic value and interest as well as pictures and furniture from the 13th-18th centuries. A 15th century fresco depicting the enthroned

Madonna and Child and a splendid 14th century Cross by the Master of Cesi are of particular interest. The collection, begun in the 16th century, was enlarged by P. Fontana and re-arranged by G. Sordini; among other works, it includes frescoes by Spagna, a "Mary Magdalene" by Guercino and several works by Alunno, Spranger and De Vecchi.

Piazza del Mercato (Market Square) - fountain.

Vicolo della Basilica, a picturesque winding alley, paved with cobblestones, typical of Spoleto.

ARCH OF DRUSUS -
The monumental arch was built in honour of Drusus, son of Tiberius. Built in the 1st century A.D., it was the entrance to the Forum.
Although it is wedged between more recent buildings, we can still admire its beauty and well-balanced proportions.

MONTERONE ARCH
(3rd century B.C.) -
One of the gateways of the ancient town walls which still remains today.

Vicolo dello Sdrucciolo ("Slippery" Lane)

ROMAN THEATRE

The theatre was built in the Imperial period and was later restored by the Romans themselves. The orchestra pit and several corridors and passages have remained intact, whereas the tiers of seating have been reconstructed over the traces of the original ones, and the stage has disappeared completely owing to the construction of the apse of St.Agatha's Church. Today, various performances are held in the theatre in the summer, as well as several concerts during the Festival of the Two Worlds (see photo).

FOTO LUCARINI

In the background is the cloister of the 11th century Convent of St Agatha where the Spoleto section of the National Archaeological Museum of Perugia is being set up. Next to the convent is the portico of the church in which frescoes dating from the 12th century can be seen.

CHURCH OF ST. PHILIP NERI
(SAN FILIPPO NERI)

The church was built in 1640 in the Baroque style. It was designed by the Spoleto architect, Loreto Scelli, on the model of the churches being built in Rome at the time. The church has an imposing façade and dome and an interesting interior, made up of three naves separated by pillars. The former monastery of the Order of St.Philip, situated nearby, today houses the town's law-courts.

FOTO DE FURIA

After visiting the 17th century Church of St. Philip Neri, designed in the Baroque style by the Spoleto architect, Loreto Scelli, on the model of churches being built in Rome at the time, let us admire the fine staircase (photo on the left) designed by U. Tarchi (1923), which closes the east side of Piazza Pianciani, and links the square to Via Fontana Secca (photo above), which is lined with medieval and Renaissance houses and is considered to be one of the finest streets in Spoleto.

TEATRO NUOVO (NEW THEATRE)

The Teatro Nuovo (New Theatre), designed by the architect Ireneo Aleandri, was built in 1864 on the site formerly occupied by St. Andrew's monastery. The inhabitants of Spoleto, being keen playgoers, had long wished for a new theatre to be built, as they found their old Nobile Theatre (now the Caio Melisso) too small. The building has a handsome neoclassical façade and a spacious interior capable of seating up to 550 spectators. Designed in a horseshoe shape, it has four tiers of boxes and a circle. The pictorial and stucco decorations are mainly the work of Giuseppe Marella. Various cultural events take place in the theatre every year, including avant-garde opera and performances during the Festival of the Two Worlds.

Narrow street in the town called Vicolo Filippo Marignoli

CHURCH OF ST. NICHOLAS (SAN NICOLO')

The 14th century Church of St. Nicholas, with its single nave in which remains of frescoes can still be seen and with its beautiful Gothic apse, is now used to host some of the performances arranged during the Festival of the Two Worlds.

In the photo below, the cloister of St. Nicholas's, made up of many-sided pillars and small columns in white and red stone. During the Festival, exhibitions and performances are arranged in the cloister as well as the church.

CHURCH OF ST. DOMINIC
(SAN DOMENICO)

Built in the Gothic style during the 12th-14th centuries, St. Dominic's Church is noteworthy for its fine doorway on the right side wall and, inside, for important frescoes and paintings. Of particular interest are the Chapel of St Mary Magdalene and a 17th century painting by Giovanni Lanfranco.

TORRE DELL'OLIO (TOWER OF OIL) - The tower derived its name from the old custom of throwing boiling oil from it for defensive purposes. The tower is part of the Pompili Palace. To the right there is another tower, dating from the 13th century, which is shorter and is decorated with a terracotta rose-window.

In the photo below right, the 19th century fountain in Via Cecili, decorated with the coat-of-arms of Spoleto and recently restored by the "Friends of Spoleto".

VILLA REDENTA
("REDEEMED" VILLA)

Reconstructed over a 17th century building towards the end of the 18th century, the villa was given its name when it became the property of the Marignoli family again, after belonging for a time to Leo XII. In front of the villa there is a fountain, with an obelisk rising from it, surrounded by extensive grounds containing imitation ruins according to neoclassical taste.

CHURCH OF ST. JOHN AND ST. PAUL (SS. GIOVANNI E PAOLO)

This small Romanesque church built in the 12th century was consecrated in 1174. Above the side door is a 13th century fresco, repainted over the original, depicting a Madonna and Saints. Inside there are interesting frescoes narrating the stories of the saints, including Alberto Sozio's "Martyrdom of St Thomas Becket", the bishop killed in Canterbury Cathedral in 1170 and canonized in 1173, "St Francis", considered one of the earliest portraits of the saint, and many other works of interest.

ROMAN AMPHITHEATRE

Used for gladiatorial events in the Roman period, the amphitheatre was transformed into a fortress by Totila. In the 13th century the arches were filled in to form shops and in the following century, much of the amphitheatre was dismantled and the stone used to build the Fortress overlooking the town. Today only a few arches remain, which can be seen from inside the Minervio Barracks.

CHURCH OF ST. GREGORY THE GREAT
(SAN GREGORIO MAGGIORE)

After visiting the Romanesque church of St. Lawrence (San Lorenzo), which was built around the year 1100 and was recently restored (1972), and contains interesting frescoes by Spagna's school, we should visit the Church of St. Gregory the Great. Situated in Piazza Garibaldi, it is dedicated to St Gregory, who together with other eminent Christians was buried here, in a small church which provided the primitive structure for the church now standing. The style of the building is Romanesque. The façade was restored in 1907, and the original three-arched window brought back to light. In front of the façade is a 16th century portico, and to one side is the baptistry, built in the space formerly occupied by a chapel. The two halves of the bell-tower were built in two different centuries; the lower half, which resembles the Cathedral bell-tower, dates from the 12th century whereas the upper half was added later, in the 15th century. The crypt is of great interest, with its five naves and three apses and its columns made from materials taken from other buildings of various epochs. The interior, thanks to recent restoration work, has regained its original Romanesque appearance, and is divided into three naves separated by columns and pillars in the form of a cross. The raised presbytery, with three apses, was restored around 1950.

The frescoes portraying the Madonna and Child and St. Sebastian, St Rocco and St. Abbondanza (1526), the small stone tabernacle (above right) and the 15th century Madonna nursing her Child (right) are all of great interest.

CHURCH OF ST. SAVIOUR (SAN SALVATORE)

The oldest church in Spoleto, St.Saviour's is divided into three naves, separated by columns connected by an architrave running above them, an unusual and attractive feature. The right nave contains an interesting 14th century fresco depicting Christ on the Crucifix (photo on left).

Church of
San Ponziano ➤

CHURCH OF SAN PONZIANO

The church and monastery complex of San Ponziano are situated on the immediate outskirts of Spoleto, beyond the Ponziana Gateway (Porta Ponziana) and the Tessino stream.

According to tradition, the complex stands on the site where the young Ponziano was martyred in the 2nd century A.D. He later became patron saint of the town.

Although the church has been subjected to numerous architectural modifications over the centuries - at the end of the 18th century the interior was radically restored - it still contains original architectural elements and decorations of great artistic interest.

The Romanesque façade, divided into harmonious proportions by ledging and moulding, the simple and elegant doorway and the rose-window, which sadly is not well preserved, are all fine features.

The crypt, similar to the one in St. Gregory's, is also interesting. Partly made with elements from other buildings, it has a cross-vaulted ceiling and is divided into five small naves, with five apses; many of the columns and capitals come from other buildings.

In the photo below we can admire one of the apses in the crypt, with frescoes of the 14th and 15th centuries: St Sebastian, an enthroned Madonna and Child, St Rocco and three other depictions of the Madonna and Child. On the right: detail of the enthroned Madonna and Child.

FORTRESS (LA ROCCA)

The construction of the imposing fortress (Rocca) dates back to the 14th century, when the Church sent its legate Albornoz to Spoleto in order to quell civil strife in the town. It was Albornoz who commissioned the building of the fortress by the architect Gattapone and turned it into a symbol of papal authority. In the following centuries, the fortress was enlarged and embellished. During the Renaissance, famous and infamous characters such as Lucrezia Borgia and her brother Cesare (the illegitimate children of Pope Alexander VI) lived there. It became not only a centre of papal power, but also a splendid court: in the 16th century, under Pope Nicholas V, its interior was transformed and made more luxurious and comfortable, probably by the architect Rossellino.

BRIDGE OF TOWERS (PONTE DELLE TORRI)

Another superb and imposing construction is the Bridge of Towers (Ponte delle Torri), which joins the hill of Sant'Elia, on which the fortress stands, and Monteluco. The bridge rests on ten massive arches which span the deep ravine below in a spectacular and impressive piece of engineering. The bridge was almost certainly built before the fortress and it is thought likely that it was designed by the same architect, Gattapone.

CHURCH OF ST PETER (SAN PIETRO)

This church is undoubtedly one of the finest and most important examples of Umbrian architecture. A masterpiece of Romanesque art, it stands out for the fine 12th and 13th century bas-reliefs which decorate a large part of its façade. The bas-reliefs depict sacred themes, with much use of symbolic figures, and indicate an exquisite taste for decoration, extraordinary narrative clarity and purity of style. The church was built in the Middle Ages over a pre-existing temple which had been dedicated to St. Peter in the 5th century

A.D. by the Bishop Achilles, who kept certain relics of the saint in it. The people of Spoleto regarded the church as their Cathedral for a long period of time and many bishops were buried in it, as can be seen from the many remains of sarcophagi and tombs which have come to light. Later, in the 14th century, the church was restored and its structure was altered completely, but the splendid façade was left intact. The 13th century Church of St.Paul (San Paolo inter vineas) is worth a visit, with its important cycle of frescoes dating from the same century.

Details of the sculptures around the doorway

MONTELUCO

Behind Spoleto stands the hill of Monteluco, offering pleasant and scenic walks through the dense woods of holm oak that grow on its slopes right up to the summit. The wood has been considered sacred for thousands of years; as far back as pagan times it was used as a place of worship to the gods and later, with the spread of Christianity, it came to be inhabited by hermits who preferred to live in isolated spots in order to meditate and pray and remain in closer contact with nature. St. Francis of Assisi visited Monteluco and founded a monastery there which was simple and conducive to meditation, like all the places where he lived. The 13th century Church of St.Julian (San Giuliano) is situated on Monteluco; the origins of the church are connected with St Isaac but the building which stands today is of the Romanesque period. In the interior, divided into three naves separated by squat columns, there are still several interesting frescoes.

Courtyard of St.Francis's monastery, with a well. According to tradition, it was St.Francis that made water flow into the well.

THE CLITUMNUS SPRINGS (LE FONTI DEL CLITUNNO)

"Hail, verdant Umbria, and you, god of the pure spring, Clitumnus!"
It is in these words from a famous ode that the Italian poet Giosuè
Carducci described this spot that so many writers of antiquity had
already praised and admired before him. The Clitumnus Springs:
an enchanting and unique spot, an oasis of exceptional beauty and
peace, filled with colour and light, a marvellous blend of so many
natural elements. The lush vegetation, mainly poplars and weep-
ing willows, is reflected in the crystal-clear waters of the little lake.
The intense colours which envelop this spot create exceptional
reflections in the lake and the atmosphere hovers on the borders
of the fairy-tale. Not unnaturally, the ancients, enchanted by this
idyllic scene, supposed that Clitumnus, a river god who dispensed
his oracles from the depths of the waters, resided here. The
Romans believed that sacrificial animals should be brought to this
spot for purification. A former Roman temple is situated nearby, a
small, graceful building which was later converted into an Early
Christian church dedicated to St Saviour.

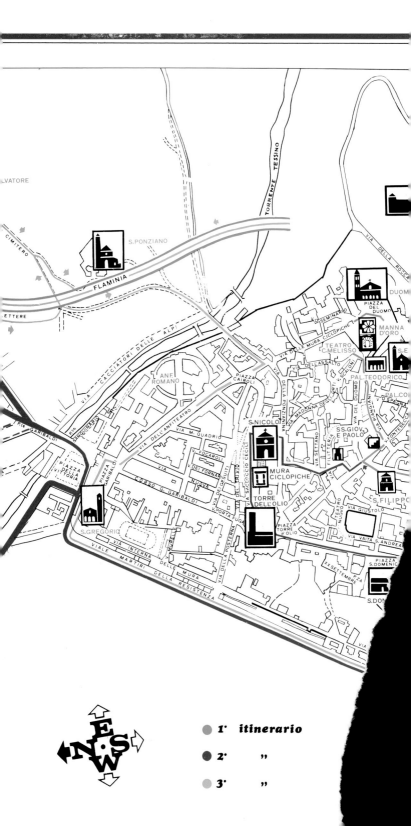

S.PONZIANO

VIA DELLA ROCCA

DUOMO

PIAZZA
DEL
DUOMO

V. SEMINARIO

MANNA
D'ORO

VIA DELLE MURA CICLOPICHE

TEATRO
C.MELISSO

VIA DELL'ASSALTO

S.E

PAL.TEODORICO

PAL.CO
D.SPAGNA

ANF.
ROMANO

PIAZZA
CAIROLI

VIA CACCIATORI DELLE ALPI

VIA DELLA PONZIANA

VIA DELL'ANFITEATRO

VIA M. QUADRIO

S.NICOLO

VIA MADONNA DE

V. FOCAROLI

VIA

V. DEI FORNARI

N.HUOVA

VIA DEL SEGUITI

VIA S.CAGGIO CECILI

MURA
CICLOPICHE

SS.GIOV
E PAOLO

VIA DI PORTA FUGA

SALVATORE

CIMITERO

FLAMINIA

ETTERE

Pte GARIBALDI

PIAZZA
DELLA
VITTORIA

SANGUINA

PIAZZA
GARIBALDI

VIA GARIBALDI

CORSO G. GARIBALDI

V.PORTA FUGA

V.PORTA POSTERNA

TORRE
DELL'OLIO

PIAZZA
TORRE
D'OLIO

VIA GIUSTOLO

S.FILIPPO

VIA DEL DUOMO

S.GREGORIO

VIA INTERNA

VIALE MARTIRI DELLA RESISTENZA

VIA DELLA POSTERNA

VIA DELLE MURA

VIA VAITA S.ANDREA

XX SETTEMBRE

PIAZZA
S.DOMENIC

S.DOM

TORRENTE TESSINO

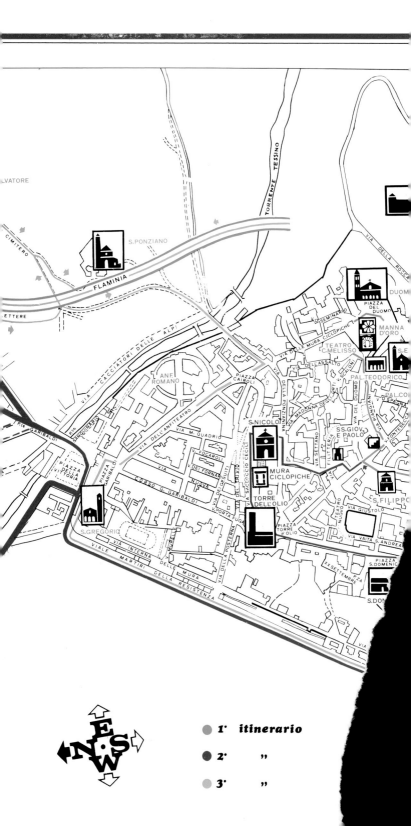

N E S W

● 1° itinerario

● 2°   "

● 3°   "

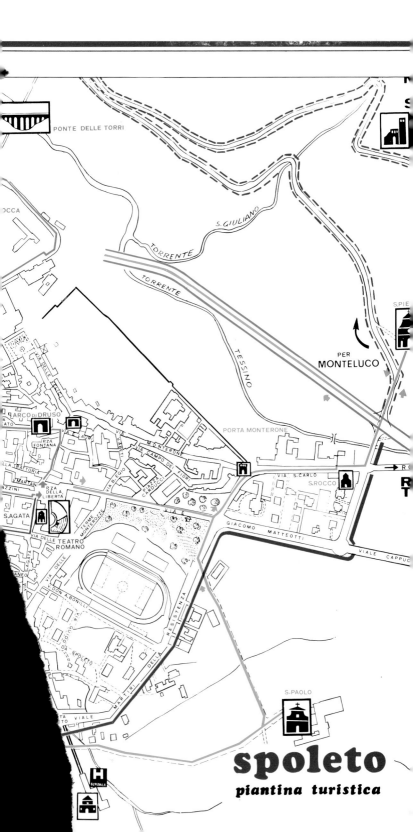

PONTE DELLE TORRI

OCCA

S. GIULIANO

TORRENTE

TORRENTE

S.PIE

TESSINO

PER
MONTELUCO

PORTA MONTERONE

VIA S.CARLO

S.ROCCO

R
T

ARCO di DRUSO

P.ZA
FONTANA

LLA FATTORIA

MARIANI

ZZINI

P.ZA
DELLA
LIBERTÀ

S.AGATA

VIA DELLE TEATRO
ROMANO

TERME
MONTROZZE

VIA

GIACOMO MATTEOTTI

VIALE CAPPUC

VIA DELLE

DON A.BONILLI

VIA

GUIDO DA SPOLETO

VIA

MARTIRI DELLA RESISTENZA

S.PAOLO

TA
O VIALE

H
B/SPEDALE

spoleto
piantina turistica

INDEX

Translated by Anita Krol